WILD
DESIGN

WILD DESIGN

ECOFRIENDLY INNOVATIONS INSPIRED BY NATURE

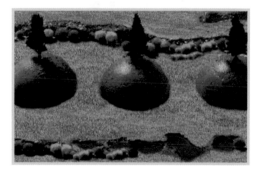

Based on the **Ecomimicry** Project

Alan Marshall

North Atlantic Books
Berkeley, California

Published by
North Atlantic Books
P.O. Box 12327
Berkeley, California 94712

Cover photo by Brad Greene
Cover photo inset by A. Marshall
Cover and book design by Brad Greene
Frontispiece art by C. Cosma and A. Marshall
Title page art by A. Revutsky and A. Marshall

Printed in the United States of America

Wild Design: Ecofriendly Innovations Inspired by Nature is sponsored by the Society for the Study of Native Arts and Sciences, a nonprofit educational corporation whose goals are to develop an educational and cross-cultural perspective linking various scientific, social, and artistic fields; to nurture a holistic view of arts, sciences, humanities, and healing; and to publish and distribute literature on the relationship of mind, body, and nature.

North Atlantic Books' publications are available through most bookstores. For further information, call 800-733-3000 or visit our Web site at www.northatlanticbooks.com.

Library of Congress Cataloging-in-Publication Data

Marshall, Alan, 1969–
    Wild design : ecofriendly innovations inspired by nature / Alan Marshall.
        p. cm.
    "Based on the Ecomimicry Project."
    Includes bibliographical references and index.
    ISBN 978-1-55643-790-8
    1. Design—Environmental aspects. 2. Art and science. 3. Art and technology. I. Title.
    NK1520.M37 2009
    745.2—dc22
                                                                    2009001858

1 2 3 4 5 6 7 8 9 UNITED 14 13 12 11 10 09

ACKNOWLEDGMENTS

The following organizations are thanked for their support of this project and publication:

Department of Environmental and Aquatic Sciences, Curtin University of Technology, Australia

Department of Ecology, Prešov University at Prešov, Slovakia

Curtin Research Centre for Stronger Communities, Australia

Alcoa Foundation, USA

Society for the Study of Native Arts and Sciences, USA

The following individuals are thanked for support of this Project and Publication:

Elizabeth Karol, Peter Manko, Branislav Hrabkovský, Jonathan Majer, Danica Fazekašová, Daniela Stehlik, Adam Dunn, Philip Groom, Brian Heterick, Nancy Spanbroek, Natasha Laurent, Richard Harris, William Parkinson.

Thanks also to Richard Grossinger, Elizabeth Kennedy, Kathy Glass, and the staff at North Atlantic Books in Berkeley, California.

All drawings and photographs are by the author or designers except where noted.

All designs are the intellectual property of the designers, reproduced here with permission.

*Radiolarian drawing
by E. Haeckel*

Radiolarian sculpture by N. O'Donovan

TABLE OF CONTENTS

Photo by Stuart Harris

Western Australian emus *(Dromaius novaehollandiae)*.

Ladybug (*Coccinella* sp.) upon a kangaeroo paw leaf (*Anigozanthos* sp.).

What Is the Ecomimicry Project?

The Ecomimicry Project is an experiment in design. The broad idea is that the natural world may serve as inspiration for design ideas. Plants and animals of all kinds have had to develop a bewildering array of survival strategies in order to cope with their life experiences. Given the great diversity of these strate gies, it is possible that there is an abundance of solutions out there in the wild just waiting to be tapped.

For plants and animals to thrive in the long term, their survival strategies usually have to be ecofriendly in some way, since a species that destroys its own environment invites future extinction. Thus, the members of the living world may offer valuable lessons in sustainability.

The concept of ecomimicry presented here is an ecofriendly and socially aware version of a discipline we might call "bio-inspired design." Often, bio-inspired design is devoted to coming up with inventions that serve industry or the military. Ecomimicry is more careful to imagine solutions that serve the environment and the community rather than the global marketplace or the armies of the world.

Carpathian Mountains of Eastern Europe.

Photo by NASA

Nature is an immense thing, both conceptually and spatially. There are many creatures to study, many strategies of survival to mimic, many stories of the natural world to emulate. Most animals and plants, though, have evolved highly specific solutions to their local survival challenges, and so the most promising source of bio-inspiration for ecofriendly design may well be the flora and fauna in the designer's own backyard. For this reason, the Ecomimicry Project concentrated on two distinct geographical regions: the South Coast of Western Australia and the Carpathian Mountains in Eastern Europe. In each region, local artists and designers, along with conser-

vationists, were encouraged to conceive of ecofriendly products, landscapes, and artworks based upon the wildlife and natural features of their region.

Many of the designs that emerged from the project are presented here, along with some works by artists and inventors who have long been inspired by the wilderness of these regions. Thus, this publication serves as a manifesto and a prospectus. It's a manifesto for designing things in an alternative way, and it's a prospectus for any future collaboration to develop the concepts further.

The two study areas for the Ecomimicry Project are far removed from each other, in both distance and character. The first, the Western Australian South Coast, is a fifteen-hundred-kilometer strip of territory trapped between the Southern Ocean and the vast arid interior of Australia.

Like the rest of Australia, the South Coast is relatively flat. The tallest spot is a place named Koikyennuruff, which stands

Bluff Knoll, Koikyennuruff, Western Australia.

around a thousand meters tall. Most of the South Coast, lies less than a hundred meters above sea level.

What the South Coast lacks in height, it makes up for in ecological diversity. There are dry scrublands in the east and exceptionally tall lush forests in the west. Many of the eucalyptus forests in Western Australia rival the coast redwoods of California in height and grandeur.

Western Australia's south is a hotspot for species diversity. Some three thousand different kinds of plants, for instance, occur only here and nowhere else.

For tens of thousands of years the South Coast was populated by Noongar Aborigines, who made a living mainly by hunting, trapping, and gathering. European settlement began with the establishment of a British colony in the nineteenth century, and now the South Coast has a mixed population of some fifty thousand people.

While it has a small population and only a low level of industry, the South Coast has nevertheless accumulated a range of environmental problems. Foremost among them is the destruction of wilderness. The main cause of wilderness loss over the

Drawing by E. Heyne

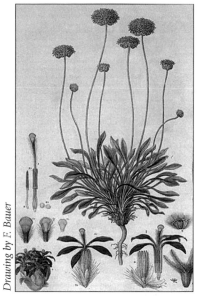

Drawing by F. Bauer

Top left: Nineteenth-century drawing of the native Balga grass trees in a Western Australia eucalyptus forest. Top right: Early nineteenth-century drawing of Australian plant *Brunonia australis*. Bottom: Jellyfish in Western Australian coastal waters.

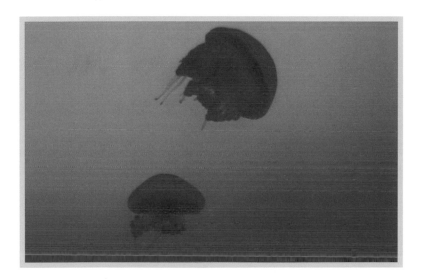

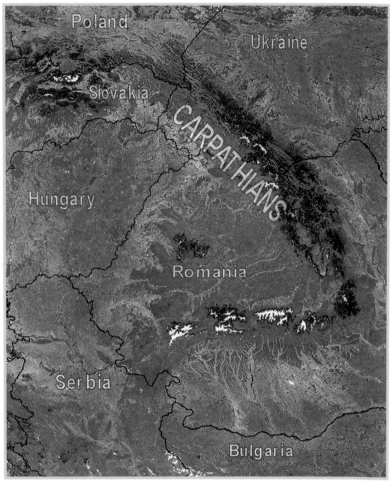

Photo by NASA

past century has been agricultural clearing, but now the damaging potential of urban sprawl and mining are becoming evident. Set against these processes is global climate change, a condition likely to compound all environmental problems. Despite these issues, the South Coast of Western Australia remains a place of enchanting wilderness, both on land and in the sea.

The second study area is the Carpathian mountain range. The Carpathians are the greatest range in Europe, traversing more than fifteen hundred kilometers and stretching through seven nations.

The nations of the Carpathians are all post-socialist states, currently transforming from communism to capitalism. The human environment of these countries is often degraded and over-industrialized, and the air and water of many towns is frequently exposed to chemical and radioactive pollution. The mountains, however, still have vast tracts of land that have avoided industrial development, usually through benign neglect rather than benevolent planning.

These untouched tracts in the Carpathians are bastions of wilderness in modern Europe, hosting large populations of carnivore species such as bears, wolves, and lynxes, while also serving as a great unbroken chain of European forest.

Left: Carpathian mountain region. Above: Kalvaria monastery, Prešov, Slovakia

The region is steeped in a unique cultural mix, too, being home to Slavs, Magyars, Romanians, and Roma, and a myriad

of smaller ethnic groups. Among these groups, and throughout European culture, the Carpathians have evoked dark legends of werewolves and vampires over the centuries.

The Carpathians begin as small hills near the Danube River in the west of Slovakia before they gradually rise up to three-thousand-meter peaks on the Slovak-Polish border.

In a great arc, the mountains then sweep through the south of Ukraine and into the Romanian landscape, where they dominate in the form of the Transylvanian Alps.

In another great arc the Carpathians then roll eastward across Serbia and—as an extension—into Bulgaria as the Balkan Range.

The mountains finally dip into the Black Sea at the Irakli Cliffs in eastern Bulgaria.

These two regions, the Carpathians and the South Coast of Western Australia, are home to the animals and plants that have inspired the designs on the following pages. It is hoped that these two regions will also one day benefit from the realization of the designs.

Serbian Carpathians, Serbia.

Balkan Range, Bulgaria.

Irakli Cliffs, Black Sea.

Product Designs

Tiger Snake Bushwear

■ **DESIGNERS:** Jan Nibbelink, Murray Ellis, Abdul Hafiz Mat Husin

The tiger snake *(Notechis scutatus)* is one of the deadliest reptiles in the world. Its venom paralyzes both muscles and nerves while also destroying the blood. Any human has about a fifty-fifty chance of surviving a tiger snake bite if not treated with anti-venom.

Photo by Bruce D. Means

It is not the offensive capabilities of the tiger snake that are of interest here, though, but its defenses. The tiger snake's scales— which may be banded, like a tiger, or blackened in color—consist of horny folds. These scales serve as a defensive layer to protect the delicate internal organs from the rough-and-tumble life of the coastal Western Australian environment. The precise overlapping arrangement of the scales also allows the snake a great degree of mobility.

The South Coast of Western Australia is a noted area of eco-tourism. High on the list of things to do is trekking in the bush near the sea. The coastal bush is not only magnificent, it is dangerous. The designers, for instance, have themselves all been bitten, cut, stung, or injured in some way by various plants and animals as they've trekked through the Western Australian wilderness. For this reason they have designed the Tiger Snake Bush-

wear, which they hope will help ecotourists enjoy being among the wildlife without being harmed by it.

The main component of the Bushwear is a full body suit, similar to the style of a wet suit or anti-mosquito wear, which serves as a light and protective garment against a potentially dangerous environment. The suit is covered by small aluminum scales that mimic the scales of the tiger snake, providing both defense and mobility. It is foreseen that the Bushwear will adequately protect the wearer from the creature that inspired the design, as well as lesser wild threats.

Twilight Beach, Esperance, Western Australia.

The Alpine Reflector Cooler

■ **DESIGNERS:** **Students from Curtin sustainable design class**

Like a monstrous alpine flower stretching for the sun, the Alpine Reflector Cooler juts out from various Carpathian buildings. The flower makes its presence visible to the world to attract pollinators. The Alpine Reflector Cooler has a different function, more like that of a canopy of leaves, which aim to catch solar rays.

A sheet-shaped cooler reflects solar radiation above a Romanian school.

The main purpose of this structure is passive cooling. The dish reflects sunlight that would otherwise hit the building below. With less solar radiation hitting the roof, it will take much less energy to keep the building cool during the summer months.

Top: A flower-shaped alpine cooler protects a public building in Transylvania, Romania. Bottom: Artistically rendered flower-shaped coolers protect a palace in Sinaia, Romania. This example attempts to blend the coolers with the architectural style of the palace.

The Carbon-Absorbing R4

■ **DESIGNERS:** Barry Patterson
and Caleb Dawson

With the industrialized world hooked on private transport, the global warming crisis might possibly be ameliorated by algae. Algae come in all shapes and sizes, and there are thousands of species in the marine environment of Western Australia.

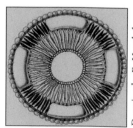

Tubular alga.

Drawing by E. Haeckel

Collectively, the photosynthetic operations of algae may possibly capture carbon dioxide at a greater rate than all the world's terrestrial forests. In view of this potential, the R4 emerges as a candidate ecofriendly vehicle, with a series of algal-filled water tubes lining the roof. These tubes act as bio-filtration units, capturing and storing carbon dioxide over a period of weeks until they are peeled off and traded in for carbon credits at service stations dotted around Western Australia's South Coast.

The carbon-storing nature of the R4 is only one of its climate-saving features. The electric vehicle is powered by four renewable forms of energy:

■ First, when parked, ribbon blades shaped like wind-dispersed seeds convert the abundant Western Australian coastal breezes into electrical energy that will be stored in a compact battery.

■ Second, electro-pedals are provided for the user, not to propel the R4, but to add energy to the battery.

- Third, a regenerative braking system that captures energy from deceleration also powers up the battery.
- Solar panels positioned between the algal strips on the roof make up the fourth form of sustainable electricity production.

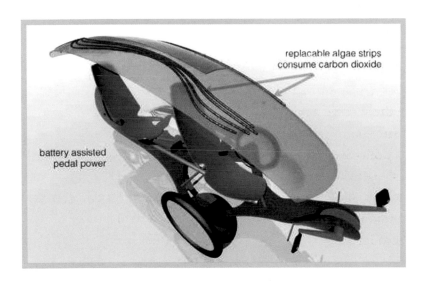

replacable algae strips
consume carbon dioxide

battery assisted
pedal power

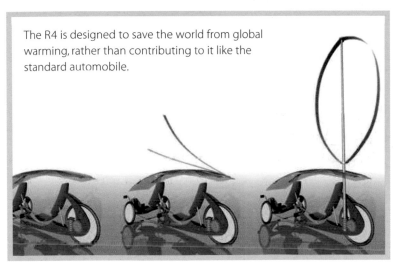

The R4 is designed to save the world from global warming, rather than contributing to it like the standard automobile.

Above: Intertidal Dwellings make up a sea village on the shore of the South Coast, Western Australia. Right: Nacre in an Australian abalone shell.

The Intertidal Dwelling

■ DESIGNERS: Curtin sustainable
design class

As the Earth's climate alters, the sea level is expected to rise as much as a meter or more. This will erode many of the prime real-estate spots in coastal Western Australia. Those Australians who believe it their natural right to live by the sea may have to think about some form of sea-worthy dwelling. The ones presented here are based on various shellfish species that inhabit the South Coast intertidal zones (areas exposed to air at low tide and submerged by the sea at high tide).

Some versions of the Intertidal Dwelling are attached fast by anchors or overhead cables in order to stay in position during surges and swells, just as some shellfish attach themselves to rocks with threads. Other versions of the dwelling are more free-floating, with only drift-anchors and buoys to keep them from drifting too far.

The material body of the Intertidal Dwelling mimics the immensely resilient nature of abalone shell, which is made up of interspersed carbonaceous and protein layers. The force of any strike is absorbed by the protein layers, allowing the carbonaceous layers to slide against each other instead of shattering. This important feature will help the Intertidal Dwelling survive the sometimes-violent oceanic weather of Western Australia.

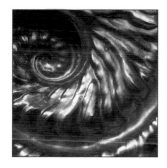

Carpathian Hairy Home

■ **DESIGNERS:** Alan Marshall
and Adam Dunn

The Carpathians are home to some eight thousand brown bears *(Ursus arctos formicarius)* spread over the forests of Slovakia, Poland, Ukraine, and Romania.

Despite the animal's name, the furry coats of brown bears come in a variety of shades. Brunettes and red-heads are quite common, and blondes, a little less so. The fur itself is very dense and provides good shelter against the elements while minimizing heat loss.

The Slavs of the Carpathians have a saying: "There's no such thing as bad weather, only a bad coat." Such is the purpose of this design: to coat the roofs and ceilings of Carpathian homes

with an artificial fur that simulates the insulation properties of the brown bear's hair. It is envisioned that the hairy home will be far easier to keep warm than standard homes during the long Carpathian cold season.

The Cephatoad Trap

■ **DESIGNERS:** Jessica Rodici, Cathy Groso, Rosanna Douglas, Emil Roskoszny

Photo by N. Martin

One night in 1935, in the tropical heat of the northeast Australian coast, a hundred and two Hawaiian-born cane toads (*Bufo marinus*) arrived in the Queensland sug arcane fields. Their job was to control cane beetles. Though dismally incompetent at this task, the imported creatures soon got on with their own goal: to colonize the entire Australian continent. Some seventy years later, the toads have spread over a thousand miles to the state of New South Wales and to the Northern Territory. They now threaten to enter Western Australia.

The Trouble with Cane Toads

- They out-compete native species for food and land;
- They exude "bufotoxins" from glands on the back of their head that harm or kill anything that tries to eat them, from domestic cats to wild crocodiles;
- They eat native frogs, birds, and insects (many of which are endangered species);
- Some bufotoxins are hallucinogenic. This property itself has led to domestic dogs becoming addicted to hunting down and thence licking the toads. A few humans have injured themselves also while partaking in this ill-advised practice.

The Cephatoad Trap, presented here, was not influenced by bufotoxins (as might be first thought) but was in fact inspired by the rare Albany pitcher plant *(Cephalotus follicularis)*. Like other pitcher plants, the Albany pitcher plant gains most of its nutrients from ants and other small insects that get trapped in its pitcher. The trap operates by luring foraging insects inside with sweet-smelling nectar. The insects can't get out due to the smooth walls and jagged lip, so they end up drowning then dissolving in the enzyme-laden puddle at the bottom of the pitcher.

Photo by G. Wardell-Johnson

Albany pitcher plants.

The Cephatoad Trap is designed to work in much the same way except on a larger scale. Instead of insects, the trap captures and disposes of cane toads. The initial lure is the flies and moths that congregate around the solar-powered light. By the time a toad catches a few of these, it has slipped into the pitcher. Over time, its dissolved remains end up fertilizing the surrounding soil.

Right: The Cephatoad Trap mimics the Albany pitcher plant in order to capture and dispose of invasive cane toads.

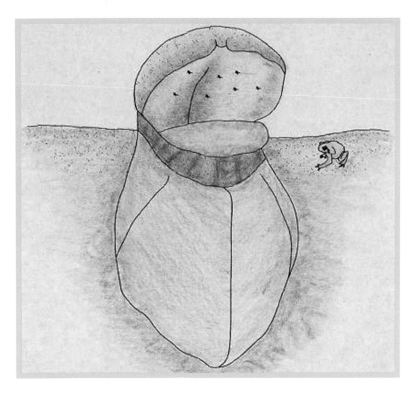

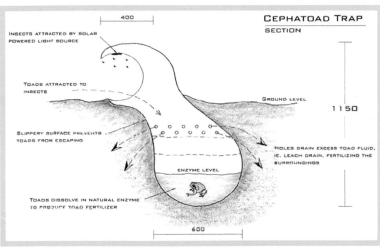

CEPHATOAD TRAP
SECTION

400

INSECTS ATTRACTED BY SOLAR
POWERED LIGHT SOURCE

TOADS ATTRACTED TO
INSECTS

GROUND LEVEL

1150

SLIPPERY SURFACE PREVENTS
TOADS FROM ESCAPING

HOLES DRAIN EXCESS TOAD FLUID,
IE. LEACH DRAIN, FERTILIZING THE
SURROUNDINGS

ENZYME LEVEL

TOADS DISSOLVE IN NATURAL ENZYME
TO PRODUCE TOAD FERTILIZER

600

21

The Malleefowl Swimming Pool Heater

■ **DESIGNERS:** April Davison, Anders Jenson, Michael Freeburn

The chicken-sized malleefowl, a native of the scrublands of southern Western Australia and named after this type of small-tree and shrub habitat (mallee), builds a most impressive nest. When fully realized, the nest can be four meters wide and over a meter tall.

Photo by Jessica van der Waag, Malleefowl Preservation Society

The nest consists of decaying leaves, within which are buried two or three eggs, covered by a huge mound of insulating sand. As the leaves decay, they produce heat, thus keeping the clutch of eggs warm. The male mallefowl precisely measures and maintains the temperature of the nest interior at 91 degrees Fahrenheit (33 degrees Celsius) by rearranging the quantity of sand on the exterior.

This design mimics the heat-production properties of the malleefowl nest for the purpose of heating a swimming pool. A heated domestic pool might be regarded as an environmentally-suspicious luxury, but the precise organic material proposed in

In a malleefowl nest, the decaying vegetation produces heat and the sand provides insulation, all to create a warm environment for the eggs nestled inside.

this design brings the pool users right back down to earthly basics, for it is the users' own bodily waste that makes up the bulk of the decaying matter.

A malleefowl-type swimming pool includes an outhouse and a glass-covered septic tank. The waste collected from the outhouse during the extensive Australian summer is encouraged to decompose when sunlight strikes the contents of the tank. The resulting natural heat is transferred to pipes to heat the pool. The user then can bathe in waters warmed by his or her own waste.

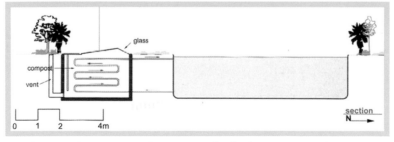

The heat producing properties of the malleefowl nest are mimicked in this pool heating system.

The Heliotropic Lodge

■ **DESIGNER:** Alan Marshall

A widespread phenomenon in the botanical world is sun-tracking—what biologists call "heliotropism." This behavioral adaptation allows plants to maximize their collection of solar rays. The most famous of the heliotropes are the sunflowers of the Helianthus family.

Drawing by Thomas Meehan

The stromatolitic rocks of Western Australia are also heliotropic. The bacteria that manufacture the rocks, such as those at Pink Lake, often do so in a slightly north-facing manner. They do this because the bacteria take their energy from the sun, which in Australia moves predominantly across the northern sky.

The Heliotropic Lodge mimics these sun-tracking plants and bacteria in order to maximize collection of sunlight. Its slightly concave, semi-circular roof is shaped to capture solar rays as the sun passes overhead. It is paneled with solar cells (and also channeled with grooves to collect rainwater). The harvested solar energy can be used to power the home and perhaps an electric vehicle, and the collected water is stored in tanks for outside use. The Heliotropic Lodge is suitable for urban areas but may reach its greatest potential in rural and wild parts of Western Australia, away from city services where energy supply and water services are unavailable or deemed too expensive.

Pink Lake, near Esperance, Western Australia.

Heliotropic house depicted in the South Coast rural environment.

Solar Petal Street Lamp

■ **DESIGNERS:** Cassandra Rowles, Bronwen Vines, *et al.*

Carpathian Version

In the morning, like a mountain flower opening to the sunshine, the Solar Petal Street Lamp opens to collect solar energy on its petalous solar panels.

Photo by P. Manko

At dusk, the petals close inwards like the very same mountain flower, and the light within the center casts its beam down, directly onto the streets of Carpathian towns, without spraying the sky with light pollution. In this way, the light from one nearby star can be collected during the day so that the light from a thousand distant stars can be seen at night.

Western Australian Version

The Western Australian version of the Solar Petal Street Lamp is based upon the flowers of native eucalypt trees.

Photo by G. Wardell-Johnson

During daytime, a band of solar cells collects light from the strong Australian sun. This energy is stored in a battery compartment within the cone. After sunset, the electricity is transferred through hundreds of energy-efficient tubules, and light is dispersed downwards to illuminate the street.

Australian Solar Petal Street Lamp in an urban environment.

The Hakea Glider

■ **DESIGNERS:** Tan Chin Leng,
John Chum, Kim Ling

The hakea trees of the South Coast of
Western Australian have vivid floral arrays
somewhat reminiscent of exploding fire-
works. After pollination, the flowers of
some hakea species produce seeds with
small wings attached. These wings help
the seeds glide in a graceful whirling mo-
tion to the ground. They also allow the
wind to send the seeds some distance away
from the parent plant, thus decreasing the
chance for competition between parent
and offspring plants.

The rise in extreme sports has provided
an opportunity for winged seeds, like those
of the hakea, to serve as inspiration for this rotating glider. In
the Hakea Glider, the pilot leaps from a precipitous perch on
the ancient granite peaks of the South Coast to descend in a
dizzying spiral to the plains below.

The Hakea Glider, an extreme sport invention, mimics the downward flight of Australian hakea seeds.

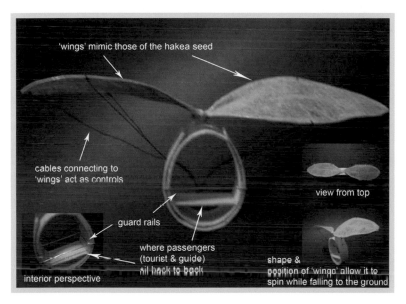

29

Hemp-Sail Battle Cruiser

■ **DESIGNERS:** Allan Riger and Alan Marshall

The Royal Australian Navy proudly adver-
tises its commitment to care for the environment, saying that it never knowingly
endangers the lives of wildlife or humans
(during exercises, it is added). For instance,
if whales or humans are swimming nearby, the Navy will desist from firing shells
in their direction.

Portuguese man-of-war,
a colonial jellyfish
(Physalia physalis).

Photo by Catherine Donker

Here is a way for the Australian Navy
to be more proactive in environmental matters. Instead of using
fossil-fuel engines, it can harness the clean energy of wind via
sails. The sails may be innovative forms based on the air-filled
bladders of the Portuguese man-of-war, for example, or they may
be of a more traditional form, like the hemp sails represented in
this design. Motorized engines would be only an emergency or
speed-needed backup.

A strict wind-power policy might be thought by some to be
an unnecessary restriction in the defense of Australia, but in the
age of dwindling oil resources, one may envision all the other
Navies of the world grinding to a halt while a wind-powered
fleet becomes dominant.

Hemp seems an appropriate material from which to construct the sails for this new ecofriendly Navy since, in its production, it uses far less polluting chemicals than most other
fibers while also being admirably durable and resistant to mold.
Some people with an ultra-conservative stance might be wary

of the mass agriculture of hemp, since they believe it will encourage mass production of the psychoactive parts or varieties of the plant. However, the military could ultimately be the main market for the psychoactive portion, since as it stands now, military doctors around the world prescribe much more expensive and dangerous drugs to servicemen whom they would not otherwise convince to return to theatres of war.

The battle cruiser in the Great Southern Ocean, with hemp sails hoisted.

Rendering of *Cannabis sativa,* a plant with multiple uses.

Toadstool Shelter

■ **DESIGNERS:** CJ De Silva, Samantha Covarr,
Claire Smith

The toadstool is the mythological shelter to
fairies and pixies in both European and aboriginal folklore. With these stories in mind, the
designers have dreamt up a shelter that can be
erected to temporarily house human travelers
in both Carpathian and Australian landscapes.

Drawing by W. Rhind

The distinct coloration of the Toadstool Shelter derives from
the hydrogel embedded in the middle layer of the cap, which
extends out to the surface at regular points. This hydrogel layer
retains water that falls upon it so that this water can be extracted
by travelers. The designers envision a transportable version of
the shelter as well, capable of folding into a pack-sized bag.

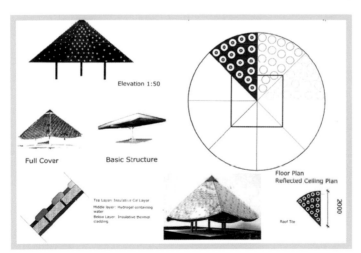

The Toadstool Shelter provides protection and water for trekkers
in the Western Australian wilderness.

The Crustacean House

■ **DESIGNERS:** Nempiris Lesiit, Cindy Lim Kow Hian, Amish Desai, Angus Macleod

Inspired by the versatile and highly functional joint system of crustacean anatomy, the designers of the Crustacean House have imagined a structure made of flexible joints. The jointed system enables the house to flex under forces and then to recover, instead of fracturing or cracking in high winds. This feature allows the structure to adapt to the potentially increasing prevalence of strong storms on the Australian coast in the era of global climate change.

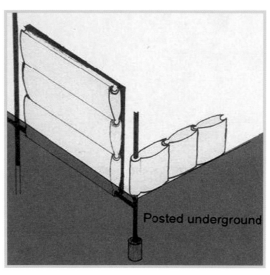

Stackable segment of the Crustacean House wall.

Crustacean Houses in the Western Australian outback.

Flying Machines

■ **DESIGNER:** Leonardo da Vinci

The art and science of mimicking Nature for technological purposes is not new. One of the most notable historical figures who scrutinized the natural world for inspiration was Leonardo da Vinci. In the 1480s, da Vinci investigated the flights of birds and bats common to European mountains before turning this knowledge into designs for flying machines.

There is some contention over whether these designs were ever field-tested, let alone proven, but they still serve to inspire the imagination of modern inventors.

Da Vinci Flying Machine, the reported inspiration for the modern helicopter.

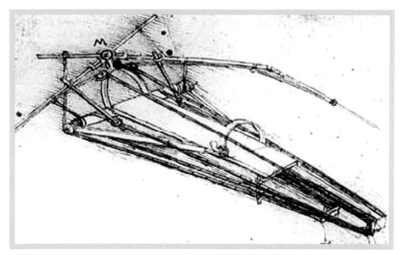

Drawing for the Ornithoptor, inspired by birds and bats.

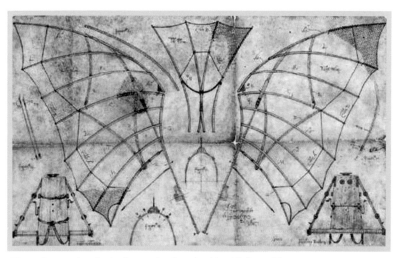

Plans for mechanical wings, also inspired by birds and bats.

37

Biomimetic Nanobots

■ **DESIGNER:** Daniel Nonnenmacher

Nanotechnology operates on the nano-scale—about one-billionth of a meter. That's about one hundred times smaller than a microscopic plant cell.

Plant stoma cells.

Photo by M. McGuire, West Georgia Microscopy Center

Various nanotech products now exist, from furniture coatings to guitar strings. Some say that nanotechnology will reach its true potential only when it is able to mimic the infinitesimal cellular bodies hidden within organisms, such as antibodies (which attack invading germs) or chloroplasts (the organelles in plants that turn sunlight into sugars).

Perhaps nanotechnology will be a boon to environmental causes since nanotech products may take on the role of degrading pollutants in the environment, ideally operating more rapidly than natural processes of breakdown. Equally likely or even more so is the possibility that any biomimetic nanotechnology will be perilous to life as we know it. Envisioned here is a nanobot (nano-robot) that has invaded the interior of a plant through one of its breathing pores. It then goes on to invade each individual cell, turning all the plant's chloroplasts into an unsightly green mush as the nanobot usurps the cell's materials for its own reproduction.

Nanobots invading a plant cell.

The Paper Wasp Tent

■ **DESIGNERS:** Susan Nguyen, Natalie Taylor, Kathryn van Vugt

Several kinds of paper wasp (such as *Polistes humulis* and *Polistes dominula*) have acclimated themselves to Western Australia in the past half century, moving in from the eastern states. While many invasive species wreak havoc upon the ecology of their new home, paper wasps may actually be beneficial (at least from the human point of view), as they prey upon numerous pest insects.

Photo by Nick Monaghan of Life Unseen

Of interest to these designers is the nest of the paper wasp. Wood and wasp-spit are the materials utilized by nesting paper wasps to construct fibrous nests comprised of numerous hexagonal cells. The entire structure is usually suspended on the underside of branches and twigs, and also under eaves and roofs.

The Paper Wasp Tent's structure is informed by that of the paper wasp nest. Here, the wasp-spit component is foregone and the tent is constructed from paper, cardboard, and plastic, all recycled. The recycled paper and cardboard give form and strength (the wood), and the recycled plastic is sprayed on as a film to provide a weatherproof coating.

The designers imagine the tent to be an easily transportable, low-cost temporary shelter with as much potential for emergency situations as for recreational use by trekkers and campers.

Photo by Nick Monaghan of Life Unseen

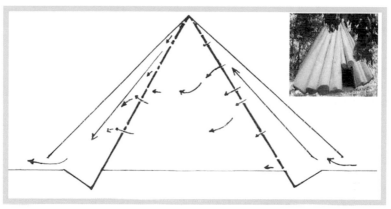

The Paper Wasp Tent with arrows showing air circulation.

Photo by Alpha Lau

The air bladders of seaweed help keep it afloat.

SkyLifter in the air.

The SkyLifter

■ **DESIGNER:** Jeremy Fitton

Seaweeds are photosynthetic, so they cannot survive without adequate access to sunlight. In order to keep them high enough in the sea to maintain contact with the sun, they possess buoyant gas-filled bladders.

The SkyLifter similarly employs a gas-filled bladder to lift it into the air. The main purpose of this invention is to serve as transportation, especially for shipping. In a flash, the SkyLifter does away with the need for extensive roads, able to carry a projected one hundred tons of goods quickly across the distant reaches of Western Australia.

As well as forsaking roads, the SkyLifter obviates the need for runways and airports since it does not land; it floats. This is highly beneficial for environmentally sensitive areas and also for under-serviced remote regions.

According to the designer, the SkyLifter is capable of moving heavy and odd-shaped items from the exact point of manufacture to the exact point of use. This helps streamline the transportation process because there are few if any relay points (and therefore few third-party transfer delays). This means reduced risk of bottlenecks and jams. Thus the SkyLifter promises a more rapid form of transport than even the fastest conventional aircraft.

The Collapsible Mallee Shelter

■ **DESIGNERS:** Students of Curtin
sustainable design class

Mallee is a type of shrubland character-
ized by small mallee trees (like *Eucalyp-*
tus eremophila). A band of mallee stretches
across the South Coast of Western Australia for thousands of miles. In North
America, the mallee counterpart would
be the chaparral of California.

Photo by S. Harris

Mallee landscapes are notorious for bushfires. As a result, tree
species must adapt to fire in order to survive. The mallee trees, for
example, possess bulbous underground stems called lignotu-
bers. After fire surges through the bush, damaging much of the
above-ground parts of the plant, buds start sprouting from the
underground lignotuber, allowing the tree to resurrect itself.

The life-saving subterranean features of mallee trees inspired
the design of this shelter system. When fire threatens, though,

Lignotuber of a mallee tree.

Photo by G. Wardell-Johnson

Like your average house in the Australian outback, most of the living space sits upon the surface (ground level).

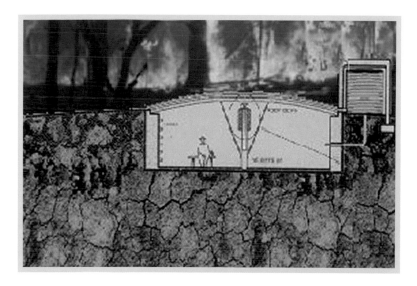

a pulley system lowers the above-ground portion into a subterranean cavity. The fire sweeps over, and when it has passed, the shelter and its occupants safely emerge.

The Crustacean Helmet

■ **DESIGNERS:** Young Kyun Ahn,
Ross Connololy, Maja Doslo

Inspiration for this bicycle helmet comes
from the many marine crustacea native to
the ocean abutting Western Australia. One
of the main functions of the crustacean
exoskeleton is to protect the delicate interior organs. Crustacean exoskeletons are
generally flexible (employing a jointed
system), and during the spawning period

Drawing by TRM Stebbing

the female is able to curl her abdomen in on itself to protect
her eggs. The Crustacean Helmet, in addition to protecting the
delicate brain, curls up on itself to provide protection from theft,
becoming a padlock.

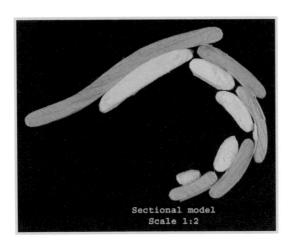

Sectional model
Scale 1:2

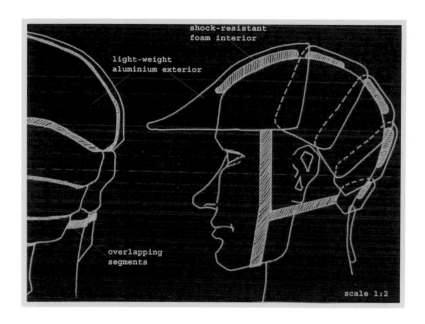

shock-resistant
foam interior

light-weight
aluminium exterior

overlapping
segments

scale 1:2

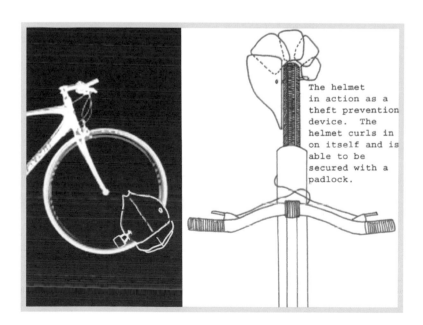

The helmet
in action as a
theft prevention
device. The
helmet curls in
on itself and is
able to be
secured with a
padlock.

47

The Reef Shark Submarine

■ **DESIGNERS: Rick Edmonson and Alan Marshall**

The waters bordering the Western Australia coast are home to
many dozens of shark species.
The reef sharks (*Carcharhinus*
spp.) are a common variety,
both in the shallow waters of

Photo by Robin Hughes

reefs and also at depths of up to a few hundred meters further
offshore. They generally feed on reef fish and mollusks and can
be quite a social animal, aggregating at the edges of reefs and
just outside lagoons. Scuba divers who frequent such environments have generally found these sharks inquisitive but non-
aggressive. Like many sharks, though, they can become dangerous
when their feeding is interrupted.

Though not a rare species, the population of reef sharks is
declining worldwide since commercial fishing fleets often catch
the sharks accidentally before discarding them as "waste."

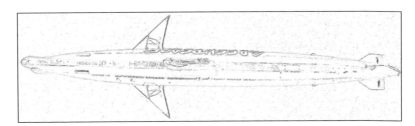

Eco-Warrior Submarine.

The sleek, hyper-efficient shape of the shark has prompted a myriad of bio-inspired designs. Here, the hydrodynamic fins and tail of the reef shark are fashioned as additions to a recycled Chinese military submarine for use by eco-warriors in the Great Southern Ocean. The shark-based features make the submarine more stable and speedy, perfect for pursuit of ecological transgressors such as illegally prowling nuclear subs, whaling ships, and environmental polluters.

The Possum Tree House, depicted in the eucalyptus forests of the South Coast.

The Possum Tree House

■ DESIGNER: Frank Godde

Western Australia has a surprising variety of possums. The so-called pygmy possums are the size of mice, while others such as the ring-tailed possum are the size of domestic cats. Most have a lush, soft, gray fur, except for the distinctive southwestern pygmy possum, which sports fur that is a delicious cinnamon color. Like their American counterparts—the opossums—Australian possums are marsupials. This means the females have pouches in which they carry their offspring during infancy. All but one species of Australian possum are arboreal, meaning they live most of their life in trees.

This Possum Tree House is designed for temporary occupation by students in the forests of the South Coast. The tree house, set some ten to twenty meters above the ground, is of particular value to students doing ecology studies on the living members of the forest community, but this design is potentially useful to students from a whole gamut of disciplines—artists and writers to architects and engineers.

Living like a possum in the canopy of a Western Australian forest has many ecofriendly characteristics compared to the traditional forest cabins built by humans:

- It allows the construction of a wilderness cabin without trees needing to be cleared;
- It exposes students more directly to the environment that they study, enhancing their observation/appreciation of the natural world;
- It teaches students to live modestly on local resources with little technological dependency.

Photo by V. Tzvetanov

Whale Boat

■ **DESIGNERS:** Baneen Khadroo,
Aisbath Zana Zubair, Mishant Patel

The waters of the Great Southern Ocean, south of Australia, serve as a favorite migration route for multiple whale species. One in particular, the humpback *(Megaptera novaeangliae)*, is a star attraction for boatloads of ecotourists, especially when the whale performs acrobatic breaches above the water line.

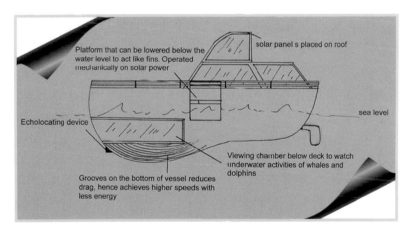

The Whale Boat is inspired by the morphology of the humpback. The boat's special features are designed to offer tourists a safe and sustainable way to view the whales above and below sea level.

The Xylemic Fire System

■ **DESIGNERS:** Emily Durkan, Hannah Gosling, Jessie Nguyen

Xylem is the network of tiny tubules that transport water through the entire internal structure of a plant. In this fire protection design, an internal network of fabric lines the inside of a house like the water-carrying xylem within the body of a tree. The fabric is intumescent—it swells 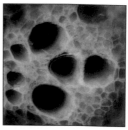 when heated, blocking off all cavities in the wall so flames cannot penetrate. The fabric also becomes doused with water, released by a sprinkler system within its membranous covering, thus acting as a cooling and wetting agent against an encroaching fire.

Photo by K. Somerville

The fabric is contained within the wall cavity by mesh and a damp-proof membrane. Excess water passes under the house and is pumped back into a tank to be recirculated. The Xylemic Fire System can be applied to just about any wall of a Western Australian building that possesses at least a few centimeters of hollow space.

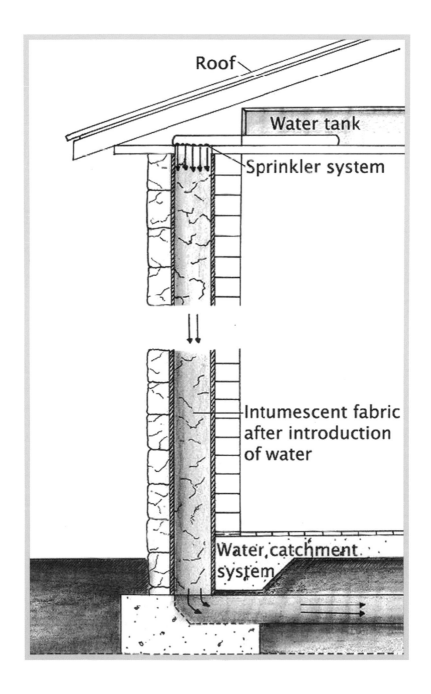

The Western Australian Ecomimicry Center

■ **DESIGNERS:** Scott Wong, Valentina Ponomariova, John McSweeney

The Ecomimicry Center aims to provide interactive education in ecology and ecodesign, as well as serving as a community center. The building is raised above the ground to avoid disrupting the land wholesale. This also allows people to observe wildlife during classes and seminars from the observation point on the second floor.

The design has some inherently ecofriendly features:

- The roof, shaped like a eucalypt leaf, is translucent to obviate the need for daytime electrical lighting;
- Storm water runs off from the roof to be collected for use in toilets;
- No car park is planned, so people will have to walk to the Center;
- It will never be built (thus avoiding any impact on the actual environment).

The Carpathian Ecomimicry Center

■ **DESIGNER:** Katka Surovkova

This design is a Carpathian version of the Ecomimicry Center inspired by a local mushroom species *(Amanita spissa)*. It incorporates the same features as the Western Australian version except that it has a car park.

The Center is designed to educate, activate, and inspire the mountain community, both locals and tourists. Along with providing training in ecomimicry, the Center's potential includes the following:

■ encourage visitors to tread lightly on the mountains while they trek or ski over them;

■ encourage locals to enroll in habitat protection projects;

■ instruct visitors and locals about the economic and ecological value of mushroom species.

Landscape and Community Designs

The Carpathian Ecosystem Swimming Pool

■ **DESIGNER:** Viktor Molnar

The term "ecomimicry" alludes to eco-friendliness in design while also suggesting that whole ecosystems might inspire design concepts. This double principle is applied here to the design of a swimming pool that mimics the ecology of a natural Carpathian lake or pond.

Photo by Darren O'Connor

Sterility is the name of the game with the average European swimming pool. Pool managers have to dump gallons of noxious chemicals into pool water to keep nasty organisms at bay, costing many hours and many dollars in upkeep—not to mention the human exposure to dangerous chemical substances.

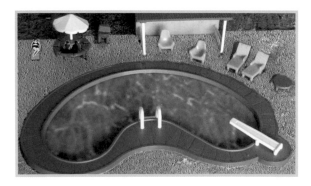

With some modifications, a swimming pool can be serviced by water-filtering plants that undertake the job of purification for free. As an added bonus, many species that grow in the pool are edible, providing a watery garden of culinary delights. The Ecosystem Swimming Pool is also able to offer Carpathian wildlife, especially rare water plants and amphibians, a home in the urban desert.

Sunk into a layer comprising about one-third of the pool are semi-submerged rocks and stones that help the plants filter the water. In the design of small ecosystems like this, there is ongoing experimentation and debate about which species best keep the pool in a state of natural balance, where troublesome organisms are discouraged and beneficial organisms are stimulated. For instance, some designers suggest that birds should not be allowed to regularly nest within the pool area because their waste will alter the chemistry of the pool to encourage algal slime and disease-causing microbes. Other designers suggest that migratory bird populations may well be tolerated if there are enough plants to filter the water.

Bat-Face Noise Barrier

■ DESIGNERS: Alan Marshall and Marek Hladik

Throughout much of Slovakia, great new highways are being eagerly approved and constructed. Primarily they are for servicing new industrial establishments, but they also serve as a throughway for skiers and tourists. The traffic on these highways produces noise pollution in the wilderness and villages of the surrounding countryside.

Slovak authorities have occasionally looked into thin concrete barriers to limit this noise pollution, but the current design goes a few steps further. The Bat-Face Noise Barrier draws inspiration from a plethora of local bat species, whose ornate facial organs are shaped to collect and disseminate sound waves.

In this design, the bat faces depicted here are scaled up in size, sculpted in 3D relief, and then mounted on the inside of an earthen barrier (facing the freeway). From the outside (the surrounding countryside), the traffic is hardly visible or audible, but on the inside, the rumbling noise is reflected back at the highway users.

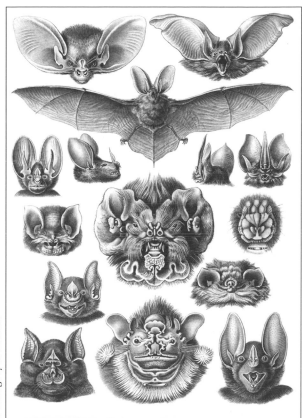

Drawings by E. Haeckel

For those road users who may regard the bat faces as hideous, the sculptures can also serve as symbolic visual reflection of the horrid noise being cast out upon the natural environment.

Beetle Bus Shelters

■ **DESIGNERS:** Desi Boshniakova, Alan Marshall, Silvia Lozeva

The insect fauna of the Balkan Range in Bulgaria have inspired this series of bus shelters planned for the local rural community. The shelters not only celebrate the local fauna of the Balkan Mountains, they enhance the value of public transport over private automobiles. Here, a snout beetle becomes a local feature in the countryside.

There are some forty thousand species of carabid beetles in the world. In the Carpathians, some kinds of carabids are particularly abundant, performing vital ecological roles such as controlling pest species. Other carabids are so rare that they have only been observed a few times  in the past two decades. This shelter aims to encourage the local people to respect the abundant ones and to keep a look-out for the rarer ones.

Rosalia alpina is a Carpathian beetle increasingly uncommon in number. Without a doubt, insects get a bad rap in the public imagination. This particular design hopes to recast the creepy-crawly label anew to elicit an image of beetles as tiny bundles of beauty.

The Jarrah Water-Recycling System

■ **DESIGNERS:** Helen Perera, Chimalizeni Mwenda, Yen Chyuan Edmond Voo

This design takes inspiration from the jarrah forests of Western Australia to propose a recycling water system for a small South Coast community. If the system can be made to operate in a continuous cycle, it will minimize waste of both water and energy.

Photo by Espen Lodden

All runoff water, along with waste-water, flows into a subterranean reservoir before passing through a micro-turbine. The power generated here subsidizes electricity supply to each home.

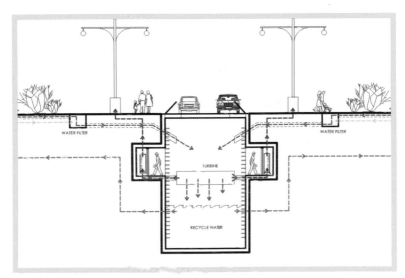

The water in the Jarrah Forest Recycling System flows through a neighborhood to hydrate, power, and cleanse the whole system in a continuous cycle.

65

The water at the lower end of the cycle then travels upward again through a pipe made of microscopic tubules. This process mimics the flow of water through the xylem vessels of plants, whereby evaporation maintains a continuous upward pull on the water. The water is then filtered by botanical stations before domestic reuse.

Like other ecological cycles, the system isn't closed entirely. More water will be added to the system from natural sources, and filtered rainwater will also flow from the system to the greater environment.

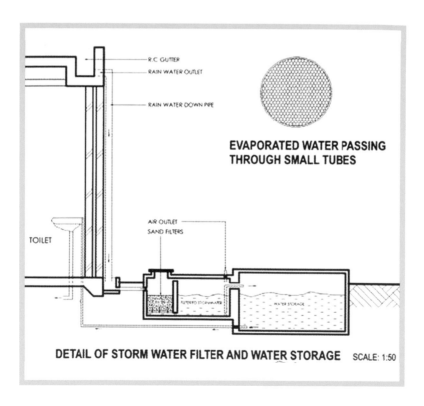

DETAIL OF STORM WATER FILTER AND WATER STORAGE   SCALE: 1:50

The Global Pathway

■ **DESIGNERS:** Zsigmund Papp,
Alan Marshall, Frank Godde

The end of the oil economy is haunting our future horizon. What are our transport possibilities in a post-oil yet thoroughly globalized world? Perhaps international travel and transport can adjust to non-motorized methods surprisingly well. To do so, we need a vast network of walkways and cycleways traversing the world. A good test of such a concept may be the design of a pathway that can bring goods and passengers from the Carpathian nations to Western Australia. Migrating animals, both birds and mammals, may well serve as a guide to constructing appropriate paths through the landscapes of Eurasia to Australia.

Pathways cutting through the forests of the Carpathians.

Some pathways may be specialized so that bicycles travel on bike paths, horses and carts travel on carriageways, and pedestrians walk on footpaths. It is possible too for the pedestrians and cyclists of the world to reclaim abandoned freeways as paths across the land. In each situation, instead of huge service stations gurgling out climate-changing fuels, multitudes of small sustainably powered stations will offer fuel for human travelers (along with maintenance of their bicycles and/or footwear).

Under such a scheme, life may be a little slower but the overall economy needn't suffer greatly, as the value of local production is encouraged over long-distance transportation of distantly made goods.

If the Carpathians are to be connected to Western Australia without the help of motorized transport, then a visionary form of oceanic travel must be developed. In this case, goods and services can be transported from Asia to Australia following the migratory paths of whale species in the Indian Ocean.

For thousands of years, the world's nations were connected by sailing ships. It's likely that these will enjoy a reprise once fossil fuels become uneconomical, traversing quietly with the whales in the seas. The cetaceans, for their part, would be most thankful since the current global fleet of motorized ships grossly interferes with their ability to communicate and navigate. A global sailing fleet would also free the marine environment from oil slicks and the chemical pollution that modern ships inflict upon it.

Drawing by Silvia Lozeva and Alan Marshall

Balkan Community Garden

■ **DESIGNERS:** Jo Ankrova
and Alan Marshall

For inhabitants of many industrial cities dotted along the foothills of the Balkan Range of Bulgaria, the mountains are a mere visual companion. They can be seen but not touched.

Most urban-dwellers here have minimal opportunity to visit the nearby mountains, so this design brings the mountain ecosystems down to the city neighborhoods in the form of a community garden.

The economic and environmental misfortune of modern Bulgarian cities has resulted in many socialist-era blocks plummeting into slum-like conditions. This design concept aims to resurrect the blocks to make them a worthwhile and satisfying home for the millions of Bulgarians who dwell within them.

The features of the Balkan Community Garden mimic the features of the nearby Balkan Range. There is, for example, an arboretum containing representative samples of mountain trees, a pond containing sub-alpine aquatic species, rooftop and school-ground plots growing local herbs and grasses, a rock garden that simulates an ancient moraine ecosystem, and a stream whose headwaters lie in the actual mountain range. Another feature is an artificial hill planted with Balkan meadow species and adorned with a miniature version of the Tsaravets Castle—a nationally famous fortress located in Bulgaria's medieval capital Veliko Turnovo. These features, taken together, would evoke a sense of ecological and cultural connection between the human community and the mountain range.

Three other aspects of the garden will encourage community involvement:

- Guerrilla gardening will be encouraged, whereby community members are free to indulge their passions in ornamental and horticultural gardening without needing a permit.
- The open spaces will help preserve the existing informal agricultural economy of the local Roma residents whose unfenced livestock (horses, goats, and cows) will provide free cropping of the grasses without recourse to mechanical or chemical means.
- Since most high schools in Bulgaria specialize in a particular discipline (technology, linguistics, etc.), it is proposed that the high school located near the garden become a specialized "ecology high school," training students in the environmental arts and sciences. The construction and maintenance of the garden may very well be part of the curricula of the school.

The Carpathian Central Nuclear Waste Store

■ **DESIGNERS:** Radko Mazanov
and Alan Marshall

It seems rather strange, but for some fans of nuclear power, the 1986 Chernobyl disaster—which continues to induce cancers in thousands of East Europeans each year—is held out as an environmental success. James Lovelock, inventor of the Gaia theory, for instance, points to the current abundance of wildlife in the towns surrounding Chernobyl as indicating that radioactive contamination and wildlife can co-exist. Because the humans were scared away by the stigma of radioactivity, the wildlife prospered. Many scientists have noted the grave genetic and anatomical damage among animals and plants in the Chernobyl-affected zone, but Lovelock is not impressed, saying that radioactivity is a natural feature of most landscapes. He believes that nuclear waste dumps should be located in nature reserves everywhere since this would stop intrusions by humans.

Chernobyl nuclear power plant, Ukraine, where a nuclear meltdown in 1986 led to massive radioactive pollution in Eastern Europe.

Photo by Ben Fairless

The design presented here takes this idea to new extremes by insisting that all the nuclear waste of the former Soviet Union be gathered and stored in one big dump in the Carpathians of the Ukraine, where the wildlife will then (supposedly) flourish for the three hundred thousand years that it takes for the radiation to decay.

Because nuclear waste facilities have repeatedly been listed as the least tolerable industrial neighbor for communities worldwide, the nuclear industry has attempted to "sex-up" its image. One way this goal has been pursued in Western Europe is by hiring artists and architects to come up with designs that add value to the facility, either by blending it into the landscape or by celebrating the technological beauty of nuclear power. The present design takes another tack, reveling in the materials of the nuclear world by proposing to construct the facility itself out of solid uranium. Why hide such a beautiful metal if it is so natural? Why not celebrate it as being a positive part of the landscape? And as can be seen here, the visible environmental benefits are profound, as the forest spreads to engulf what humans are too scared to live next to.

The designers acknowledge that this is a rather risk-laden piece of architecture, but the most accepted alternative—to dump the waste a thousand meters underground—only delays contamination of the environment by some few dozen years until fires or floods bring the waste back to the surface.

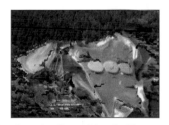

Left: Surrounding wilderness at the time the Carpathian facility was constructed. Right: The same facility fifty years later, with a visible increase in surrounding forest.

Australian Eco-Golf

■ **DESIGNERS:** Angus Mcleod
and Alan Marshall

Golf courses worldwide have a substantial, even disastrous environmental impact upon their local environment. A multitude of sins follow their spread across the globe:

- They overuse water, siphoning it off from natural ecosystems and more essential services.
- The pesticides and herbicides used on golf courses run off to damage ecosystems downstream.
- Their construction and maintenance involve destruction of natural habitat.
- They encourage an over-abundance of exotic ornamental plants which can escape and become weed species.
- They impede the flow of mobile and migratory species across the landscape.
- They discourage ecological diversity in favor of uniform landscaping.
- They encourage long-range vehicular transportation. People travel for many miles to hit around a small dimpled ball.
- They grease the social networks of the corporate elite, easing the way for future plans of destruction.

For those who wish to continue the sport, here's the ecofriendly alternative. Walk to your nearest vacant or degraded lot with a couple of clubs, and bash around a ball. If you attract the interest of the local authorities, ask them to join in, explaining that what you are doing is a community-oriented and ecofriendly form of golf. With a little bit of luck, they may think twice about granting the local golf club a new license until it learns to create a course that mimics the natural landscape. In the case of Western Australia, it would be something like this design.

Marine Algae Harvesting System

■ **DESIGNER:** Daniel Nonnenacher

With the looming spectre of climate change there is no guarantee that terrestrial agriculture can supply the world with all the food that it needs and the bio-fuel that it craves. The damselfish may provide inspiration to overcome this situation. Some damselfish are algae farmers, cultivating a single favorite alga, *Polysiphonia*. The fish busily weed their *Polysiphonia* plots of competing seaweeds, and they actively scare away grazing fish.

In this design, a biomorphic algal farming device searches for new algal spores to fill its tanks before joining a central station that pumps "seaweed juice" to consumers on the Western Australian coast.

Marine Algae Harvesting System in the Great Southern Ocean.

Biosphere 3

■ **DESIGNERS:** Milos Farkas
and Alan Marshall

Biosphere 1 is the Earth—or to be more precise, the thin sphere of air, water, and land on the surface of the planet where most life can be found.

Photo by NASA

Biosphere 2 is a bold experiment in the Arizona desert that aims to mimic the original biosphere. It is composed of a series of grand greenhouses within which are embedded representative mini-ecosystems from various parts of the planet.

In the operation of Biosphere 2, there were numerous problems with closing off the internal environment from the external environment. Ambient gases kept entering, and carbon dioxide built up on the inside. Small creatures also kept crawling in and out, and given the runaway imbalance of some of the ecosystems, many of the essential plants and animals died.

Biosphere 2,
Arizona, US.

Photo by R. Thomas

Because of these problems, an improved design, Biosphere 3, to be set in a Carpathian valley, is proposed here. This design accepts the impossibility of sealing off a portion of the living planet from the rest of the living world. Therefore, a great big hole is left open to allow all manner of creatures (birds, mammals, insects, microbes) to enter and exit.

One of the reasons for undertaking research into self-contained artificial ecosystems like Biosphere 2 is to eventually set them up as bases on the Moon and planets. However, it may well be the case that ecological systems can't be so contained. Biosphere 2, for example, suffered from explosions of pest species, the death of pollinators, and a disrupted horticultural system. Thus, such artificial biospheres may doom astronaut settlers to starvation and asphyxiation in uninhabitable, sludged-up fish tanks.

Flying Squirrel Walkway System

■ **DESIGNERS:** Pavlo Antonov and Alan Marshall

Flying squirrels are now absent from the Carpathians, being restricted in Europe to the forests of northern Finland and Russia. However, their mode of travel through the forest is highly relevant for modern planners in Carpathian cities. The flying squirrel climbs to the upper reaches of trees then leaps off, unfurling its furry membrane to glide to another tree up to fifty meters away.

In this design, the squirrels' gliding pattern is mimicked in the form of walkways that convey pedestrians between levels of urban structures. The gliding strategy of the flying squirrel enables it to move about the forest without being vulnerable to surface-dwelling predators. In a similar way, walkways connecting tall buildings allow city dwellers to traverse their surroundings without descending to the dangerous and over-polluted surface (where automobiles speed dangerously through the streets while spewing out toxic chemicals). If such a walkway is

Drawing by F. Siebold

constructed, it will be possible for city residents to get from one side of the inner city to the other without having to contend with the horrors of the traffic below.

Some urban planners in North American cities have suggested that every yard of skyway decreases motorized traffic in a proportional manner since people decide to leave their cars at home. This may not be a conscious decision but an unconscious acknowledgment that the city center is more accessible and habitable when you can avoid all the jams, noise, exhaust fumes, and other time-consuming stresses and dangers of the street.

Carpathian Wild Park

■ **DESIGNER:** František Petrovi

Nestled within the Ukrainian Carpathians near the Polish border are the decaying remnants of a wooden church and its gardens. This design resurrects the gardens as a wild park—a park that will mimic the various ecosystems of the Carpathians, from upland forests and lowland woodlands to meadows and wetlands. Within

the park will be the myriad creatures that inhabit these ecosystems. Except for external barriers of reclaimed stone walls from the monastery set up on the perimeter of the park, there are no enclosures. Human visitors will trek upon the pathways with no division between them and the wildlife. This type of embedded ecotourism exposes human travelers to the thrill and danger of a real wildlife situation and also resurrects the human role in Nature as potential source of prey for carnivores like bears and wolves.

Gondwana Link

■ **DESIGNERS:** Keith Bradby, Amanda Keesing, *et al*

In the past fifty years, great swaths of native vegetation have been cleared in southern Western Australia to make way for agriculture. Because of the area's rich diversity and its high number of endemic species (creatures that occur in only one place), this loss of native vegetation amounts to an environmental catastrophe. The Gondwana Link project aims to resurrect the ancient woodlands and shrublands of this part of Australia by preserving remnant stands of native flora and connecting them through re-vegetation of the agricultural landscape between them. The

Image courtesy of the Wilderness Society, Australia

The southwestern portion of Western Australia, showing the vast tract of land that the designers hope to re-vegetate with native forest and shrublands.

Gondwana Link project thus acts as a grand design to mimic the original precolonial landscape.

In the illustration we can see Gondwana Link in action: A piece of untouched wilderness stands behind an agricultural area that has recently been re-vegetated. It is hoped that the ecological processes of the primordial woodland will soon start taking effect, and the rare animal species will thereby have a larger natural area to call home.

Photo by A. Keesing

According to the designers, the greatest threat facing the remaining wildlife of southern Western Australia is fragmentation. Although land-clearing has halted, the current wild areas are too fragmented to compose a sustainable ecosystem. Until these areas are reconnected they will continue to lose even common species since there are too few food opportunities in each isolated spot, too few safe areas from predators and global warming, and too few chances for each species to mix genes. The Gondwanalink designers hope to bridge the barriers between the isolated wild zones so that animals and plants can move and migrate with ease throughout the entire southern part of Western Australia.

Industrial Ecology Mining Operation

■ **DESIGNER:** Daniel Nonnenacher

There are plenty of industrial designers working under the auspices of "industrial ecology," trying to get the cycles of industry to mimic the cycles of Nature so that both exist sustainably together. The present design, however, suggests that, at least in the mining sector, the processes of ecology cannot possibly be emulated in industry, because neither humans nor Nature have the ability to absorb and break down the million of tons of unnatural waste that the mining industry produces.

Some processes just can't be made a part of the natural ecosystem, and the gold-mining practice of mixing cyanide with crushed rocks is one of them. The illustration shows a decay-

ing Western Australian gold-mining design where the biomorphic shape of the mining operations wasn't enough to save the landscape and the workers from suffering the effects of cyanide pollution.

The design also serves as a pointed reflection toward a specific gold-mining disaster that links the Carpathian nations with Australia. In January 2000, a tailing pond in Eastern Europe owned by a Western Australian mining company burst its banks to release 100,000 tons of cyanide and other deadly chemicals into the Tisla and Danube rivers of Romania and Hungary. The resulting contamination wiped out fish, birds, and mammals all along the lower reaches of the Danube to the Black Sea, as well as shutting off water supplies for millions of human residents.

The derelict skeleton of a biomorphic gold-mining facility in the Western Australian outback.

Arcological Towers

■ **DESIGNERS:** Milan Hodža and Angus Mcleod

Arcology is a style or type of mega-architecture with an ecological bent. Advocates of arcology consider their megastructures to be the perfect antidote to urban sprawl. An arcological tower requires about two percent as much land as a typical city of similar population. With little need for cars or massive roadways, such megastructures may also give rise to positive environmental rehabilitation.

Other people, though, might say that such megastructures are enormous monuments to planned societies that would envelop the individual in an abominable techno-prison. The obvious riposte is that the car and the suburb have already imprisoned us in a technological nightmare, but because they avail us with greater personal space, we equate them with freedom.

Arcological Tower depicted near the High Tatras, Slovakia.

Whatever the case, if arcology is to be a viable eco-architecture, then it must be place-based to some degree, and the two designs here make some effort toward that. The Carpathian example has rings of horticultural plots circling the towering central column. The crops cultivated in these concentric gardens gradually change with altitude, thus mimicking the stratified bands of vegetation on the nearby mountains.

The Western Australian design is located offshore in order to survive the environmental challenges that climate change will bring and to enable an easier shift to an algal bio-fuel economy.

Offshore arcological towers depicted in the Great Southern Ocean, south of Western Australia.

Balga Mud Village

■ **DESIGNER:** Jay Gardney

The long-term future of the towns and cities of Western Australia is in serious doubt. When climate change ravages the landscape beyond the capacity to support mega-cities, the human survivors will have to downscale and learn to live on the last remaining local resources. According to this design, two reliable resources will be balga trees (*Xanthorrhoea* sp.) and mud. Here, survivors of an ecological tragedy build their houses out of mud, sourced from the nearby earth and mixed with dried plants and dung.

Balga mud village set in the Western Australian landscape.

The mud may serve as infrastructure, but the future economy in general is based on the cultivation of balga, a long-living tree adapted to the dry Australian environs. The balga can supply the skilled cultivator with all manner of products and services. The resin, for instance, can be used as an adhesive in tool-making, the floral nectar provides for a sweet drink, and the floral spike can make a great fishing spear.

Photo by Barbara Harris

Alive, sea urchins are covered with an array of formidable spines. When desiccated and denuded, the striking radial structure of the sea urchin is exposed. With warm dead seas lapping at the future Western Australian coast, there may be plenty of sea urchin skeletons lying around to serve as inspiration for the shape of the mud huts.

Photo by Tom Weilenmann

Carpathian Wildland Ski Park

■ **DESIGNER:** Mikail Paulinyi

Ski resorts have a profound environmental impact, causing damage to or stress upon the local wilderness. The Carpathian Wildland Ski Park attempts to allay some of these impacts by setting

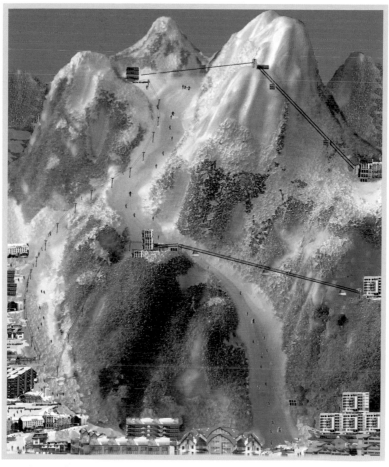

Rendition of modern Carpathian ski resort.

Carpathian Wild-
land Ski Park.

a strip of montane forest within the ski slopes. The precise mix of species in the strip will mimic the tree community of untouched Carpathian highlands (including various pines, spruces, and beeches).

A typical ski slope is denuded of trees. Pictured above, a stock of trees native to the area has been cultivated. This doesn't make the slopes less ski-worthy, only a little more challenging. As well as having to slalom through the trees, skiers forego motorized ski lifts. Instead they are to trek along ascending paths with their skis upon their backs.

Cattle Siting System

■ **DESIGNER:** Traditional

According to traditional wisdom within Carpathian villages, the best place to set up a new building, be it a home or a church, is the exact place where a respected cow or bull rests. The cow or bull is going to choose only a warm and dry resting place after all, and therefore the place chosen will give an indication of the driest and warmest micro-site in the area.

Photo by Catherine Donker

New Martian Carpathia

■ **DESIGNERS:** Antoni Gorski
and Alan Marshall

For many, Mars is but a cold, rusty-red
rock in space. Nonetheless, the Red Planet
has served as an inspiration for countless
cosmic dreamers. Science fiction writers
and astronautical engineers have imagined Mars terraformed into a new Earth,
replete with landscapes and settlements
mimicking their favorite spots on Earth.
In this design, the entire Martian sphere
is transformed to mimic the Carpathian
region, with sub-alpine woodlands growing around the volcanic peaks, and lowland forests in the valleys and plains.

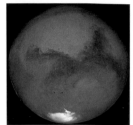
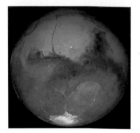

Photo by NASA

If such efforts prove to be successful, Mars would be rendered into a green utopia, with a hint of mining and industry to supply the folks back home with important resources.

The chances of this grand plan being brought to fruition may be very low, given some of the dubious technological processes involved in terraforming. Some engineers plan to seed the planet with genetically engineered algae that release oxygen from the rocks to create a breathable atmosphere. Others think such a process will take too long, on the scale of thousands of years, and instead they plan to "nuke" Mars, liberating oxygen quickly from the Martian substrate. Still others plan to construct gigantic orbiting mirrors to reflect sunlight onto the surface to warm it up.

Fortunately or not, these ambitions are floundering since nobody at the moment is able or inclined to pay for terraforming. Space mirrors and interplanetary nuclear bombs don't come cheap. But if some valuable mineral deposit is found on the Red Planet, all this may change and a Martian gold rush would likely ensue. The end result would be a grand mockery of utopia, with all the worst features of the Carpathian landscape in evidence: industrial wreckage, polluted waterways, contaminated land. This design concept below portrays such a dystopian Mars, replete with unearthly mutant plants, crashed space mirrors, and radioactive rivers.

Eco-Anarchic Governance

■ **DESIGNERS:** Peter Kropotkin *et al.*

Leaderless societies abound in Nature. According to nineteenth-century Russian revolutionary Peter Kropotkin, they are worth emulating in the human realm. Such societies would not be nihilistic and chaotic but symbiotic and mutualistic.

The usual argument for the presence of a government is that societies would fall apart into some depraved and individualistic "Wild West" scenario—a battle of "all against all." According to eco-anarchists, however, this wouldn't necessarily be the case since natural cooperation and symbiosis will allow effective localized organization of societies.

In such a design, the governments of Australia and the Carpathian nations would be disbanded, and in their place volunteer working groups would be set up to deal with particular public projects, including, for example, projects on sustainable design.

Photo by S. Harris

Many animal societies—bird communities included—exhibit cooperation and mutual aid.

Under eco-anarchism, the power of the State would default back to the people. With the State's ability to raise massive revenue taken away, national armies and armories would crumble and decay, and the world would become a far more peaceful place.

99

Carpathian Recycled Tower

■ **DESIGNERS:** Cornel Cosma and Alan Marshall

Photo by Mike Quigg

Among the many abandoned industrial projects in post-socialist Romania are remnants of half-finished grandiose structures like hydropower plants. The Carpathian Recycled Tower is a pointer to the possible use of the physical remains of such projects: a vertical village as tall as a small mountain. This is no planned tower, like that dreamt of in arcology, but an unplanned, organically organized, communal dwelling fashioned together informally.

One of the great lessons of ecology is recycling. All "waste" is used again somehow. When creatures die, their material remains are recycled by scavenging insects and microbes that carry out the work of decomposition. The Recycled Tower is a testament to the power of recycling.

Within the Carpathian nations there are some eight million Roma people, an ethnic group often referred to as Gypsies by

English-speakers. Romanians are usually at pains to make sure foreigners understand that Roma and Romanians are ethnically distinct, the former having origins in ancient India and the latter having a mixed Roman and Thracian heritage.

According to popular myth within the Carpathian nations, the Roma are responsible for inordinate damage and destruction to public buildings, including their own State-built housing. Another popular story about the Roma is that they are dealers of garbage. More often than not, this story is cast about to admonish the Roma lifestyle, which is often segregated from the mainstream wage system. In these environmentally sensitive times, however, garbage recycling has become an honorable activity. The Carpathian Recycled Tower design aims to communicate the idea that the Romanian government should hand over the decaying infrastructure of their abandoned white elephants to the Roma people. This will give an opportunity for the Roma to show how they can build communities in their own way. They can surely do no worse than a lot of government projects.

Above: Teasel Banksia sculpture. Right: Drawing of Teasel Banksia *(Banksia pulchella)*.

Art from Ecomimicry

Teasel Banksia Series

■ **DESIGNER:** Nuala O'Donovan

When eighteenth- and nineteenth-century European botanists investigated the wildlife of Australia, they came across bizarre new plants that only superficially resembled those of their homeland. To make sense of these novel species in their own

Drawing by F. Bauer

minds and that of their audience back home, they gave the Australian plants European names like "Australian pine" and "Australian she-oak," even though the species were totally unrelated.

The teasel banksia is another example: Superficially looking like the teasel grasses of Europe, it is actually a plant that occurs only in Australia. Artist Nuala O'Donovan draws upon both natural history traditions, Australian and European, to construct an archetypal teasel form (shown at left) that marries the continents under one aesthetic moment.

"Banksia"

■ **DESIGNER:** Eugene Chattelle

It's hard to overstate the fascination and affection that modern Western Australians have for the banksia tree. For artist Eugene Chattelle every part of this tree is a wonder of Nature's design— its unique form, angular serrated leaves, magnificent candle-like flowers, and beautifully sculptured nuts. "Banksia" acknowledges this affection in a reverential artwork. Banksia leaves were exposed onto cloth using a sun-dyeing technique, and the images were then hand-painted and stitched with a variety of felts.

The woodlands and heathlands of Western Australia are home to at least sixty varieties of banksia. The archetypal floral spike of a banksia looks like a brightly colored bottle-brush pointing to the sky, boosting the popularity of this species as a garden plant throughout the continent. Banksia are also popular among the native wildlife as a food source due to their abundant nectar. All sorts of animals (from pygmy honey possums to fruit bats to countless Australian insect species) use banksia as a primary or secondary food source. Alas, some banksias are now becoming endangered, and this obviously does not bode well for the animals that depend on them. As a partial response, some conservationists are attempting to popularize the rarer species as worthy ornamental plants so that their future may be secured in urban gardens if not in the wild.

The Romanian Atheneum

■ **DESIGNER:** Albert Galleron

The current interest in natural design in the environmental movement is hardly a first. In the late nineteenth century, the Art Nouveau style was predicated on mimicking natural forms. This style is richly represented in a number of major urban buildings in the Carpathian nations, including the Romanian Atheneum, home of the Bucharest Symphony.

Gilt pine cones within Romanian Atheneum, Bucharest.

Exterior of the Romanian Atheneum, Bucharest.

Interior detail of the Romanian Atheneum, Bucharest.

Carpathian Peace Park

■ **DESIGNERS:** Andreas Revutsky
and Alan Marshall

On the border between Slovakia and the Ukraine an impermeable wall of wire and electronic surveillance is being assembled. Because Slovakia has recently been admitted to the European Union, while Ukraine languishes in a post-Soviet economic nightmare, Slovakia has become the first barrier against a westward surge of illegal immigrants. Because of this, the Slovak government has been given hundreds of millions of euros by richer European nations to line its eastern frontier with electronic detectors.

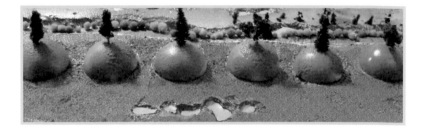

The present design is a counter to this heightened state of division between Slovakia and the Ukraine. It is a peace park that straddles the border between the two countries. The park consists of a green walkway following a natural waterway, as well as a strip of earth mounds representing various Carpathian mountains that are part of the two nations. Each mound has a familiar Carpathian tree species rooted at its peak. It is hoped that by the time the trees reach maturity, the borders between Ukraine and Slovakia will be more permeable and friendly, so that the word "visa" isn't uttered in terror.

The chances of Ukrainians enjoying free passage are not great for the near future, but the park also acts as a corridor for mobile non-human species between the Slovak and Ukrainian parts of the Carpathians. If nothing else, such a corridor may show how free the Carpathian wild animals are, compared to humans.

The Cone Series

■ **DESIGNER:** Nuala O'Donovan

With cavities and scales, infolded, reversed, and with negative space brought into positive relief, both European and Australian cones are investigated through O'Donovan's work.

Cones from various Carpathian and Australian species.

Cone sculptures (fabric).

The Black and White Mountain Sculpture, Parts I and II

■ **DESIGNER:** Ion Breton

During the communist era, many Carpathian mountains were regarded as no more than untapped reservoirs of natural resources, most notably metallic ore, water, and wood. Nestled within the Transylvanian Alps of Romania, for example, numerous towns became industrial cities, while the areas surrounding them became dumpsites for industrial waste. Far from being a place of pristine Nature and fresh mountain air, certain Carpathian mountains were just as likely shrouded in smog and dark soot. The Black

and White Mountain Sculpture, Part I, reflects this unfortunate industrialization of the landscape with soot-covered mountain-pyramids.

Part II of the design is a representation of the Carpathians in the capitalist era. Nowadays the Transylvanian Alps have become the home of multinational gold prospectors and the playground for Western skiers and Dracula romantics.

Agro Art

■ **DESIGNER:** Nik Schnieder

The artworks presented here depict agriculture in both Carpathian and Western Australian environments. Their sameness is palpable. This is both comforting and frightening. The world's culture and economy are reassuringly based upon the same tastes and values, but this fact also means that diversity has been trampled under uniformity as agro-industrial empires sweep the globe.

Wheat: A ubiquitous organism in the world's agricultural ecosystems.

Photo by M. Passon

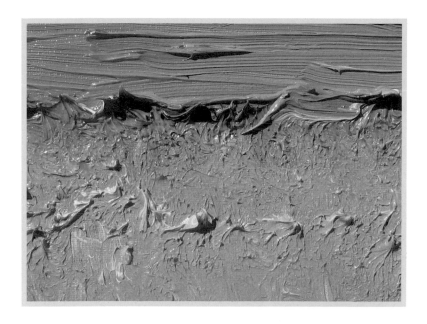

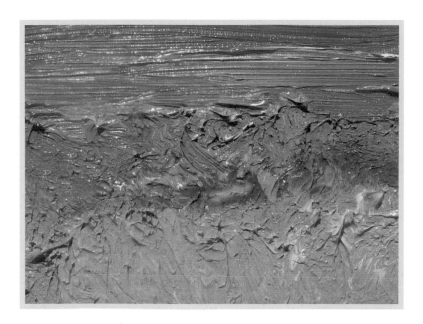

Fireseeds Series

■ **DESIGNER:** Matthew Harding

Many Western Australian trees have evolved with periodic forest fires, to the extent that their seeds are only released from seed pods after being exposed to the extreme heat of a fire. This

strategy allows new seedlings to avoid competition with established plants, enabling them to colonize the open ash-laden ground beneath a burned-away sub-canopy.

The Fireseeds are an artistic reminder of this process, showing the exuberance of seed dispersal and germination in the wake of what seems like a catastrophic natural event to human observers.

The Human Animal

■ **DESIGNER:** Tomáš Hrůza

The Czech wilderness serves as the environment for this performance by a human animal. Stripped of artifice, *Homo sapiens* looks awkward yet keen and adaptable, as though resistant to—but at home within—the rest of the ecological world. Is Hrůza suggesting that we go back to Nature (to mimic the natural world completely)? Or is he suggesting that we are actually forever a part of Nature (that everything we do mimics something natural)?

Perhaps also there's another comment embedded in this artwork: that humans now are merely unwieldy tourists when we seek to enter Nature—and we are doomed only to parody Nature when we attempt to mimic it.

Chrysalis Cycad Lamps.

Chrysalis Cycad Lamps

■ DESIGNER: Adam Cruickshank

These bioformic lamps mimic the overlapping leaves of Western Australian cycads, ancient plants whose adult form bears visual similarity to palm trees. The cycads are also reminiscent of the spiral form of a chrysalis, the pupal stage of a butterfly.

Like the mature form of cycads and the transitional shape of a chrysalis, the lamps have had to evolve into position slowly. The cycads and chrysalis achieve this through evolution and morphogenesis, and the lamps through the eager crafting of sheets of varnished cardboard.

Carpathian Wabi-Sabi

■ **DESIGNERS:** Various

Photo by G. Monteforti

Wabi-sabi is a Japanese aesthetic, one with special appreciation for the beauty of transience and decay. "Nothing lasts, nothing is complete, and nothing is perfect." This refers just as much to human designs as to Nature's designs, and it also reflects upon the imperfection of the art and science of mimicry.

A Carpathian version of *wabi-sabi* would identify quite well with the notions of transience and decay because so many life-changing events have affected the people of this region in modern history (invasions, wars, revolutions). For them, transience and transformation seem ever-present.

While transience and decay may provoke pessimism (since people are often powerless to halt change), it can also promote a sense of hope (since the next situation to come along might be a little nicer than the situation today).

According to the Carpathian mindset, the animal and vegetable creatures that grow on human artifacts, that survive industrial degradation and reclaim a life from it, are worthy of admiration. We humans do our best to control Nature but sometimes, perhaps at the moment when our structures seem permanent and everlasting, wild life will penetrate their cracks before eventually breaking them all into fragments and dust.

Radiolarian sculpture by N. O'Donovan

Radiolaria Fabric Series

■ DESIGNER: Nuala O'Donovan

Amoebae with skeletons. That is the brief description of radiolaria—microscopic creatures that comprise a large bulk of the world's animal plankton.

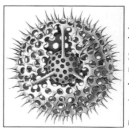

Drawing by E. Haeckel

At left, radiolarians from the Southern Ocean are dissected and reconstructed, offering up a new skeleton for modeling these tiny but ecologically significant creatures.

Animal plankton are a vital link in the Southern Ocean as they are for all oceans, serving as intermediaries in a grand food web between the oceans' vast array of plant plankton (which they usually consume) and larger organisms such as fish and marine mammals (which the animal plankton feed).

Plastic and Perge Installations

■ **DESIGNER:** John Dahlsen

Dahlsen's playful extrusions have a serious message. The works here analyze recycling and waste, questioning the recyclability of something as noxious as plastic.

Plastics degrade very slowly, releasing toxic fumes as they do. The humble plastic bag also destroys wildlife by strangling— plastic bags are responsible for 100,000 mammal deaths per year in the USA alone, entangling and choking seals, dolphins, and otters on coasts and waterways. The bags have also been implicated in devastating floods worldwide, since they clog up urban drainage systems during wet weather.

Dahlsen's response, his organic blobs, mimic the liquidized nature of plastic's source material: oil. His Perge installations signify the need for us to expunge the conveniences of plastic from our daily life. Why must we strangle the natural world, and wage oil wars across the globe, just because we lack the imagination to bring our groceries home in an ecofriendly way?

Cadmium Yellow Perge installation

Shadow Tree

■ **DESIGNER:** Matthew Harding

To be in the shadow of a tree is serene. The harsh light of the Western Australian sun is muted and dappled, making one happy to be amongst Nature.

To be in the shadow of a tree when no tree is around is a catastrophe, as though some environmental bomb has gone off, denuding the landscape and leaving nothing but wistful traces of something now absent—along with the burning sun in one's face.

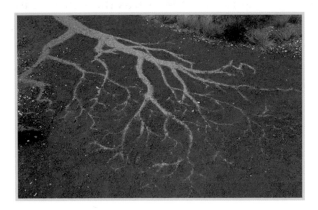

Slovak National Monument

■ **DESIGNERS:** Olyssia Krestan
and Alan Marshall

The Slovak nation came into formal existence in the 1990s. Many leaders of the nation lament the woeful level of public exuberance over a unique Slovak identity, and this design plays with these issues. The five peaks of the adored High Tatra range serve as inspiration for this monument, which is to be set within the lower gardens of Bratislava Castle.

Each peak has a trickle of water descending from it which, when exposed to the winter weather, turns the surrounding grounds to ice, making the area perfect for eager kids to play ice hockey, the Slovak national game.

Photo by Sylwester Stelmach

This gaudy nationalism takes a stark turn after about half a dozen winters. The sculptures are designed to fracture: each peak will break in two, with one third of the granite mountain falling away to smash onto the ground.

Despite Slovak pride in their mountain landscape, the High Tatras do not belong to Slovakia alone—they are set within Poland as well. This sculpture fractures the collective identity of Slovaks whose nascent nationalism overstates the distance between themselves and their close neighbors.

The Slovak National Monument, depicted five to six years after installation.

Plastic Sea Creatures

■ **DESIGNER:** Helle Jorgensen

Jorgensen recycles plastic waste into wondrous forms. The first design presented here is a nautilus, a rare visitor to southern Western Australia but common in the tropical northern part of the state. Although related to the octopus, the nautilus is a much more ancient being, surviving like a living fossil for millions of years. And where an octopus looks well-endowed with eight arms, nautilus species can possess up to ninety. The other obvious difference is the shell, a chambered external skeleton that allows the nautilus to descend to depths of up to eight hundred meters.

The second work is your archetypal stinging jellyfish. Western Australia is home to numerous dangerous jellyfish, especially a variety of deadly cubazoans (like *Chironix fleckeri* and *Carukia barnesi*). This work might be seen as a memorial to Nature's propensity to deliver fragile beauty and potent danger together; or it might be an acknowledgment that, despite all their surfing and swimming, Australians do not have complete reign over their marine environment

Forest Meeting Point
■ **DESIGNER:** Cecile Williams

Williams's design might be classified as environmental art, a genre that promotes sensibility to place. Environmental artworks exude ephemeralism instead of monumentalism. They tread lightly on the Earth but can weigh heavily on the emotions.

In this piece, moments of first contact are commemorated. Williams has particular fascination for the contact between European and Aboriginal women in nineteenth-century Western Australia. This piece alludes to other situations as well, prompting thoughts about the random convergence of all mammalian forest dwellers—for example, the initial moments of hesitation when visual contact is made, through fear, curiosity, enchantment, and hope. If, somehow, fear and aggression don't come to the fore, tolerance can flourish and the chance of future friendship may emerge.

Shells from the Sea

■ **DESIGNER:** Anna Gunnardottir

These sumptuous tactile interpretations of marine life have adorned the suburban sands of a Western Australian beach during a sculpture festival, as though washed up by a spring storm. Their generic forms, made from natural dyes on wool, remind one of various Western Australian cone shells (*Conus* spp.).

Although these artistically rendered shells seductively invite one to touch them, this is probably not the best idea when it comes to real cone shells. The cone shells of Western Australia are home to large carnivorous sea snails capable of spitting venomous harpoons on their predators and prey. They have been recorded to fatally harpoon human beings, since there is no known anti-venom.

Photo by Dagslyós

Casuarina Sculpture

■ **DESIGNER:** Matthew Harding

The Western Australian casuarina tree *(Casuarina obesa)* is wispy in appearance, reminiscent of some northern-hemisphere pines. The casuarina possesses fine feathery leaves (like the casuari bird that lends its name to the tree) and a wood often used for the making of boomerangs. What interests artist Matthew Harding here, however, are the forms of the casuarina fruits.

The fruits are also of interest to the red-tailed black cockatoo. If you are on the lookout for one of these rare parrots, the best thing to do is keep very quiet and listen for the sound of casuarina seeds being cracked open in the treetops.

Along with possessing a subtle beauty and considerable ecological value, the rather uncelebrated casuarina has a potentially important future in Western Australia. It is able to withstand both drought conditions and wet weather and is resistant to the increasing saltiness of Western Australian soils. It also provides a satisfactory timber. Thus, any program of revegetation in outback Australia may well rely on this tree.

The Starfish Series

■ **DESIGNER:** Nuala O'Donovan

As geometrically sweet as they are to the human eye, the central mouth of the Australian starfish might regarded with a certain sense of dread.

Starfish are predators with a propensity for shellfish, which they envelop in a

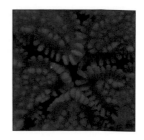

deadly embrace before injecting one of their two stomachs in between the gaps of the shell.

The starfish stomach dissolves the flesh of the shellfish *in situ.* The dissolved flesh is then brought back into the central mouth, leaving only a shell to wash up on the Western Australian coast.

Sea Urchin Pottery Series

■ **DESIGNER:** Melissa Bridgman

These stoneware sea urchins are designed to be engaging in a tactile sense. The ones that are almost too spiny to touch are the designer's personal favorites, as though the very hands-on process of making the pottery is also a way to render the finished product untouchable.

Photo by Aurora Jayne

The Emergence of Scientific Truth

■ DESIGNERS: Silvia Lozeva
and Alan Marshall

For thousands of years the origin of European glass eels remained a mystery. Aristotle believed that infant glass eels emerged prolifically out of the earth itself. Recent scientific research reveals that the eels actually swim to the waterways of Europe all the way from the Sargasso Sea in the Americas, a three-year-long journey across the Atlantic Ocean and then into the Mediterranean and Black Seas. Unfortunately, the species is now threatened by climate change, overfishing, and pollution. As this artistic design forebodes, at the moment when scientific truth emerges, wild creatures may be doomed to death and extinction.

In other words, we may rejoice in the human capacity for scientific progress, but all too often— as demonstrated by the petrified young eels—scientific progress is accompanied by an increased capacity to destroy the natural world.

Traditional Carpathian Craft Designs

■ **DESIGNERS:** Various craftsmen, including
Igor Mihailescu

The use of flora and fauna in decorative design reflects a time-less human fascination with Nature. The woodcraft and ceramics of the Carpathians are especially rich in this tradition, which dates back well before medieval times. The artistic origins of such designs are so distant that modern craftspeople can hardly retrace them.

These pieces, from Transylvania, were crafted recently from local wood. They combine age-old floral motifs with nineteenth-century veneer techniques. Similar motifs appear on woodwork throughout Transylvania—for example, on wooden grave markers, wooden gates, wooden cutlery, and the wood trim around doorways.

Photosynthesis Enhancement Installation

■ **DESIGNER:** Hui Wai Keung

In this installation, the artist aims to visualize and amplify the relationship that humans have with trees. Oxygen masks descend from the trees to transfer the much-needed by-product of photosynthesis directly to a human consumer. The similarity to airliner emergency masks alludes to our planet's gas exchange woes, where elevated carbon dioxide levels in the atmosphere are gravely threatening both trees and humanity.

Coral Sculpture Series

■ **DESIGNER:** Nuala O'Donovan

The coral life of Western Australia is the starting point for the 3D fabric sculpture below. This particular piece reflects not just the generalized form of one species, but the structure of a particular individual specimen.

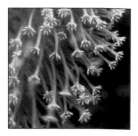

The exact shape of coral specimens often depends heavily on the personal histories and life encounters of each creature, including effects of natural forces and their various confrontations with other organisms. This uniqueness is mimicked in O'Donovan's work. From it we can observe a strong sense of adoration for the imperfect form, and the necessarily plastic nature of biological forms as they adjust to a dynamic environment.

Shell Sculpture

■ **DESIGNER:** Matthew Harding

Washed-up shells, broken and shattered, signal the abundance and diversity of Western Australian marine life. Beneath the crashing waves of the serene beaches of the South Coast are grand natural communities comprised of numerous different species. This artwork makes the life in the seas more tangible for landlubbers.

The Carpathian Monument

■ **DESIGNER:** Gary Tonge

The first image in our journey of ecology-inspired designs, the Tiger Snake Bushwear, envisioned that certain members of the natural world are out to attack us. Now, in our closing design,

we seek to honor the harmonious majesty of Nature via a mountainous life-size monument.

Such a monument is as enchanting as it is frightening. If we ever have the will or the way to mimic the grandeur of entire mountains, it is probably only because we've developed the technological capacity to destroy them as well.

Reflections

A wiser person than I might not have used the categories "Products," "Landscape and Community," and "Art" to divide this book into sections. I say this because all industrial products are actually part of a landscape and a community. All products have origins in the land or the sea, and their materials flow back there eventually, as they break apart and decay. Products also originate from communities, arising from particular intellectual traditions that nurture them, particular policies that mandate or permit them, and from social settings that make them possible or necessary. Similarly, the "Community and Landscape" and "Art" designs presented in these pages are themselves "products," being—as they are—packaged concepts seeking to be sold and/or consumed within a marketplace of ideas. And, of course, all the designs in the book can be considered pieces of art, seeking to inspire and challenge us with hopes and fears of our environmental future. Thus expressed, each design brought into this book possesses a technical, social, and artistic character beyond what is immediately visible.

The Ecomimicry Project has given rise to many imaginary techno-gadgets. At the same time, it has asked many of the student designers involved to inspect the role of technology in the environmental crisis. Some of the works showcased in this book have an irreverent approach to modern technology, declaring it a fetish that is killing the world. Other designs suggest that technology may be important in the search for ecological solutions but, in and of itself, it's not the whole answer. In order to avoid environmental catastrophe, we have to look more widely, beyond technological solutions, into the hearts and minds of people and the relationships between them and Nature.

As acknowledged earlier, Nature is an immense thing, both physically and conceptually. The designs that emerged through this project, now presented within this book, all reflect differing stories about Nature and how it might be emulated. Some people see Nature as a creative force, some as a peaceful paradise, others as part of our human identity. A number see it as rather alien and unknowable, yet also endlessly enchanting. The one common attitude, though, that permeates most of these designs is this: they embody a reflection of the endangered circumstance of Nature's members in the modern world. Because of this, these designs either aim to change the world or they are designed for a world that has changed.

If the industrialized world is to survive, then most environmentalists believe some reconciliation with ecological principles is vital. In the Ecomimicry Project this has involved casting Nature into the role of both mentor and muse. But what exactly does it mean to learn from the natural world? Does it mean we emulate technologically solutions found out there in Nature, or could we learn from less technical (more generic) principles, like rebirth and recycling? In this project, both approaches have led to insightful, and often rather playful, results.

However, before congratulating ourselves upon our own cleverness (and thinking humans are the only ones capable of ecomimicry), we need to pay yet another homage to Nature. The phenomenon of biological mimicry, where one organism mimics another, has been a part of the living world long before humans were around to fashion their first tools. A native of the Western Australian coast, the leafy sea dragon—with its amazing seaweed-like camouflage—reminds us of this.

Photo by Sean Harrington

BIBLIOGRAPHY

Aldersley-Williams, H. (2003) *Zoomorphic: New Animal Architecture.* London: Laurence King Publishing.

Ausubuel, K. *et al.* (2004) *Nature's Operating Instructions: The True Biotechnologies.* San Francisco: Sierra Club Books.

Benyus, J. (2002) *Biomimicry.* New York: Perennial.

Dorf, R.C. (2001) *Technology, Humans and Society: Toward a Sustainable World.* Orlando, FL: Academic Press.

Edgar, J. (2006) *Wild Australia: A Guide to the Places, Plants and Animals.* Sydney: Reed New Holland.

Farkas, Z. & J. Sos. (2007) *Transylvania: A Land Beyond Fiction and Myth.* Budapest: Jel-Kép.

Hammer, N. (1999) *Interior Landscapes.* Beverly, MA: Rockport Publishers.

Hemenway, G. (2001) *Gaia's Garden: A Guide to House-scale Permaculture.* White River, VT: Chelsea Green Publishers.

Koren, L. (1994) *Wabi-Sabi for Artists, Designers, Poets and Philosophers.* Berkeley, CA: Stone Bridge Press.

Laurenza, D., M. Tadei, and E. Zenon. (2006) *Leonardo's Machines: Da Vinci's Inventions Revealed.* Newton Abbot, Devon, UK: David and Charles Publishers.

Lefroy, E.C. *et al.*, eds. (1999) *Agriculture as a Mimic of Natural Ecosystems.* Dordrecht: Kluwer Academic Publishers.

Lewis, H. *et al.* (2001) *Design + Environment: A Global Guide to Greener Goods.* Sheffield, UK: Greenleaf Press.

Littlewood, M. (2005) *Natural Swimming Pools.* Atglen, PA: Schiffer.

Martin, D. (2006) *Nanobiotechnology of Biomimetic Membranes.* New York: Springer.

Mollison, B. (1988) *Permaculture: A Designer's Manual.* Stanley, UK: Tagari Press.

Neill, W. (1993) *By Nature's Design.* San Francisco: Chronicle Books.

Porteous, C. (2002) *The New Eco-architecture.* New York: Taylor and Francis.

Poole, B. (2006) *Green Design.* New York: Mark Batty Publ.

Roberts, J. (2005) *The Mountains of Romania.* Milnthorpe, UK: Cicerone Press.

Soleri, P. (1999) *Arcology: The City in the Image of Man.* Phoenix, AZ: Bridgewood Press.

ABOUT THE AUTHOR

Alan Marshall is an environmentalist and an academic. Much of his career has been devoted to heavily criticizing environmentally dubious technologies. After writing and talking a lot about the way modern technology destroys both human and non-human communities, Alan finally took the advice of friends and colleagues, to stop being so cynical and offer an alternative. The Ecomimicry Project is the result, a three-year project that sought to offer artists and conservationists a way to express their own technological futures. For Alan, the Project was one of "bringing together," since it combined his passion for science with his passion for art and design; it brought together his research and teaching experiences in Eastern Europe with his experiences in Australia; and it merged his desire to democratize technology with his desire to conserve Nature.

Alan has a bachelor's degree from the University of Wolverhampton (England), a master's degree from Massey University (New Zealand), and a doctorate from the University of Wollongong (Australia). He has held fellowships at various universities in Australia and Europe, including Curtin University of Technology (Australia), Masaryk University (Czech Republic), and the Institute for Advanced Studies in Science, Technology and Society (Austria).

Alan's other books include:

Lancewood (Indra Publishers, Melbourne, 1999)

The Unity of Nature (Imperial College Press, London, 2002)

Dangerous Dawn: The New Nuclear Age (Beyond Nuclear
    Initiative, Melbourne, 2006)